TORNADOES!

WILD EARTH

BY MARCIE ABOFF

ILLUSTRATED BY ALEKSANDAR SOTIROVSKI

Consultant: Susan L. Cutter, PhD
Director, Hazards and Vulnerability Research Institute
Department of Geography
University of South Carolina, Columbia

CAPSTONE PRESS
a capstone imprint

First Graphics are published by Capstone Press,
1710 Roe Crest Drive, North Mankato, Minnesota 56003.
www.capstonepub.com

Books published by Capstone Press are manufactured with paper
containing at least 10 percent post-consumer waste.

Library of Congress Cataloging-in-Publication Data
Aboff, Marcie.
  Tornadoes! / by Marcie Aboff ; illustrated by Aleksander Sotirovski.
    p. cm.—(First graphics. wild earth)
  Includes bibliographical references and index.
  Summary: "In graphic novel format, text and illustrations explain how
tornadoes form, how they are measured, and how to stay safe during one"—
Provided by publisher.
  ISBN 978-1-4296-7608-3 (library binding)
  ISBN 978-1-4296-7952-7 (paperback)
  1. Tornadoes—Juvenile literature. I. Sotirovski, Aleksandar, ill. II. Title. III.
Series.
  QC955.2.A25 2012
  551.55'3—dc23   2011028743

Editorial Credits
Christopher Harbo, editor; Juliette Peters, designer;
    Nathan Gassman, art director; Kathy McColley,
    production specialist

Printed in the United States of America in Stevens Point, Wisconsin.
102011   006404WZS12

Table of Contents

Tornadoes 4

Spotting Tornadoes 10

Staying Safe 16

Glossary 22

Read More 23

Internet Sites 23

Index 24

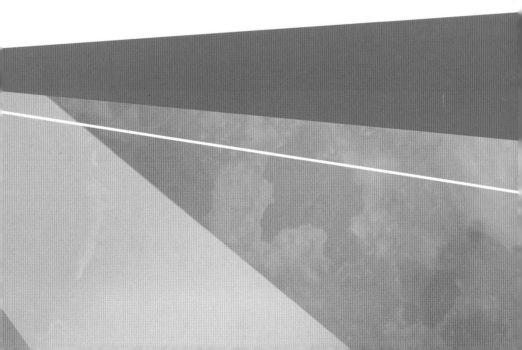

Tornadoes

A strong thunderstorm rolls across the plains.

Suddenly a funnel-shaped cloud stretches toward the ground.

The swirling cloud races across the land.
It destroys everything in its path.

This spinning column of air is a tornado.

Tornadoes form in very strong thunderstorms. Strong thunderstorms form when cold air meets warm, wet air.

The cold air lifts the warm air. The rising air meets rotating winds that create a funnel cloud.

When a funnel cloud touches the ground, it becomes a tornado.

The United States, Europe, and Southeast Asia have the most tornadoes.

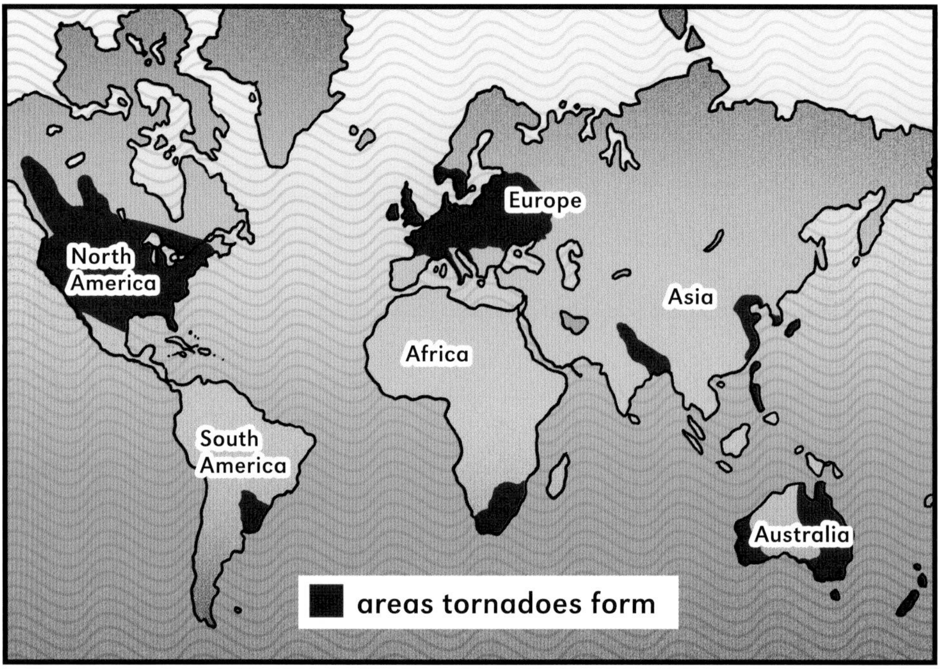
North America
Europe
Asia
Africa
South America
Australia
areas tornadoes form

In the United States, more than 1,200 tornadoes form each year.

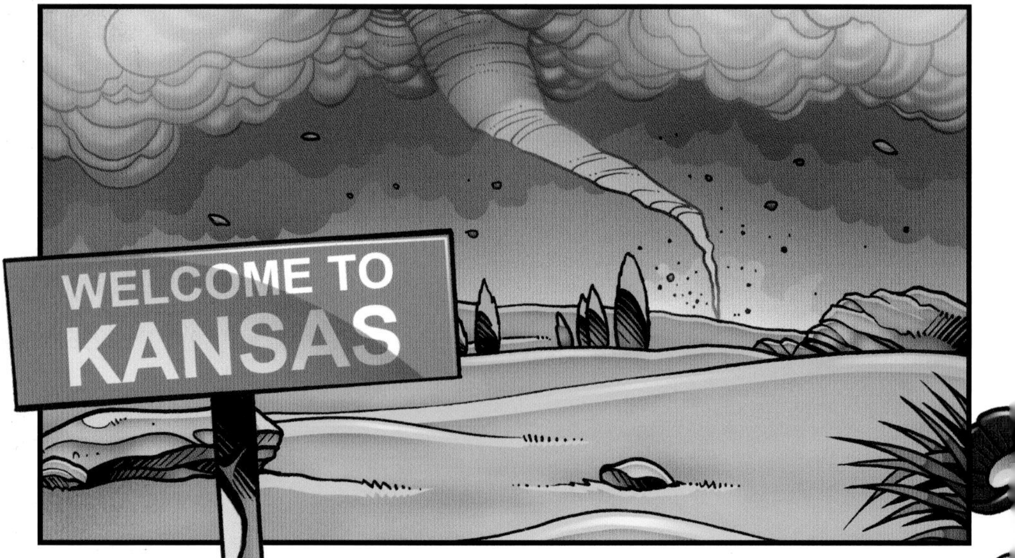
WELCOME TO KANSAS

Most of these tornadoes happen in the central and southern states. This area is known as Tornado Alley.

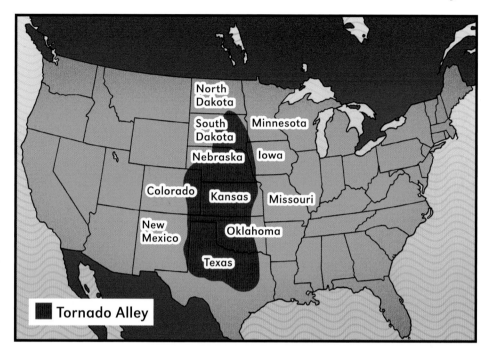

North Dakota

South Dakota

Minnesota

Nebraska

Iowa

Colorado

Kansas

Missouri

New Mexico

Oklahoma

Texas

Tornado Alley

Tornado Alley gets most of its tornadoes between March and August.

Spotting Tornadoes

Weather forecasters and storm spotters watch for tornadoes.

Forecasters use weather radar to watch thunderstorms. Radar shows changes in a thunderstorm and where a thunderstorm is going.

Storm spotters watch thunderstorms from the ground. They spot tornadoes as they form.

Scientists rank a tornado's strength on a scale.

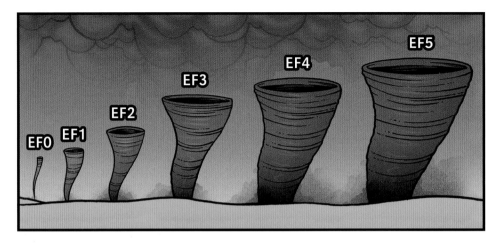

The higher the number, the more damage a tornado can cause.

Weak tornadoes break tree branches and damage houses.

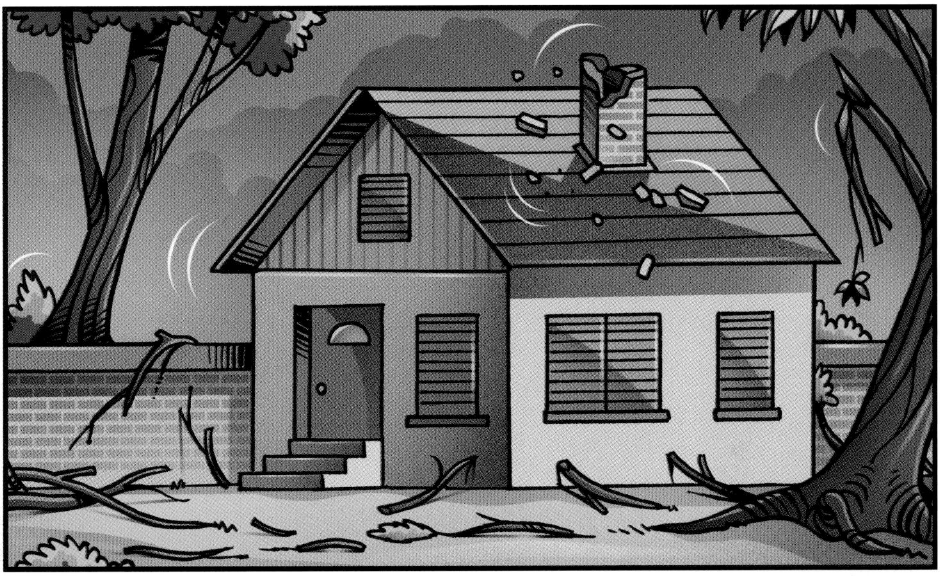

They are strong enough to push cars off the road.

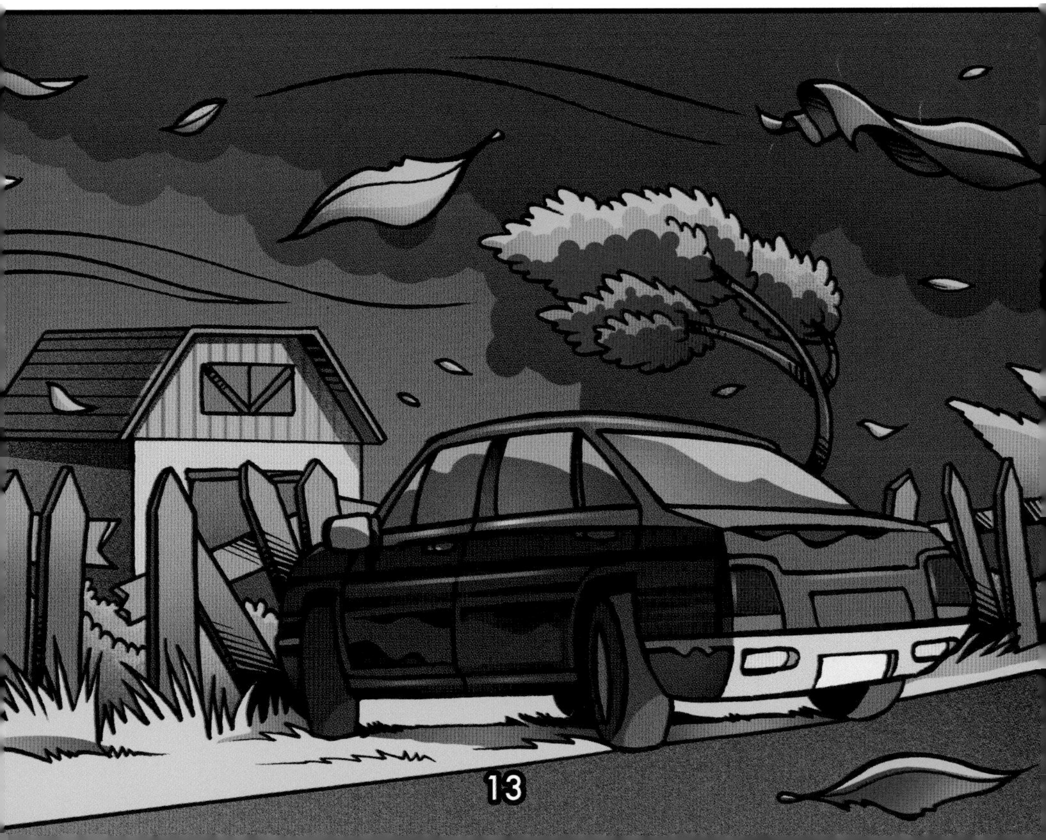

Strong tornadoes tear the roofs off houses and push over large trees.

They can also tip over trains.

The strongest tornadoes pick up cars
and snap trees in half.

They completely destroy houses and other
large buildings.

Staying Safe

Tornado safety starts with listening to weather reports.

Weather forecasters sometimes issue tornado watches and warnings.

A watch means a tornado could form.

A warning means a tornado has been spotted in the area.

People stay safe by knowing where to go when a tornado strikes.

A basement is the safest place to be during a tornado.

If you don't have a basement, go to an inside room on the lowest level. Stay away from windows.

During the storm, crouch down on your knees. Protect your head with your arms.

To stay safe, make a tornado plan with your family.

Know where to find a battery-powered radio
and flashlight.

Practice where to go and what to do during a tornado.

Being prepared when a tornado happens will help you stay safe.

Glossary

forecaster—a person trained in weather science who reports on weather conditions

funnel cloud—a cone-shaped cloud that is usually a visible part of a tornado

radar—a weather tool that sends out microwaves to determine the size, strength, and movement of storms

rotate—to spin around

scale—a series of numbers that is used to measure something

Read More

Bodden, Valerie. *Tornadoes*. Mankato, Minn.: Creative Education, 2012.

Rebman, Renee C. *How Do Tornadoes Form?* Tell Me Why, Tell Me How. New York: Marshall Cavendish Benchmark, 2011.

Schuh, Mari C. *Tornadoes*. Earth in Action. Mankato, Minn.: Capstone Press, 2010.

Internet Sites

FactHound offers a safe, fun way to find Internet sites related to this book. All of the sites on FactHound have been researched by our staff.

Here's all you do:

Visit *www.facthound.com*

Type in this code: 9781429676083

Super-cool stuff! Check out projects, games and lots more at **www.capstonekids.com**

Index

funnel clouds, 4–5, 6–7, 11

radar, 11

safety, 16–21
scientists, 12
storm spotters, 10–11

thunderstorms, 4, 6, 11
Tornado Alley, 9
tornadoes
    damage from, 5, 12–15
    formation of, 6–7
    locations of, 8–9
    seasons for, 9
    strength of, 12–15

warnings, 16–17
watches, 16–17
weather forecasters, 10–11

Titles in this Set:

EARTHQUAKES!

HURRICANES!

TORNADOES!

VOLCANOES!